ELIZABETH I

First paperback printing 2007
First published in North America in 2005 by the
National Geographic Society
1145 17th Street N.W.
Washington, D.C. 20036-4688

Paperback ISBN: 978-1-4263-0172-8
Hardcover ISBN: 978-0-7922-3649-8
Library ISBN: 978-0-7922-3654-2

Design: Two Associates
Series editor: Miranda Smith
Picture research: Caroline Wood

For Marshall Editions:
Publisher: Richard Green
Commissioning editor: Claudia Martin
Art director: Ivo Marloh
Picture manager: Veneta Bullen
Production: Anna Pauletti

For the National Geographic Society:
Director of Design and Illustrations:
Bea Jackson
Project editor: Priyanka Lamichhane

Consultant: Dr. Lucy Wooding is a lecturer in Reformation history at King's College, London.

One of the world's largest nonprofit scientific and educational organizations, the National Geographic Society was founded in 1888 "for the increase and diffusion of geographic knowledge." Fulfilling this mission, the Society educates and inspires millions every day through its magazines, books, television programs, videos, maps and atlases, research grants, the National Geographic Bee, teacher workshops, and innovative classroom materials. The Society is supported through membership dues, charitable gifts, and income from the sale of its educational products. This support is vital to National Geographic's mission to increase global understanding and promote conservation of our planet through exploration, research, and education.

For more information, please call 1-800-NGS LINE (647-5463) or write to the following address:

NATIONAL GEOGRAPHIC SOCIETY
1145 17th Street N.W.
Washington, D.C. 20036-4688 U.S.A.

Visit the Society's Web site at www.nationalgeographic.com.

Previous page: In this picture from a 16th-century manuscript, Elizabeth I sits on the throne in her royal robes.

Opposite: This painted wooden crest was placed in a church during Elizabeth's reign. It symbolizes the position of the monarch as governor of the Church of England.

Printed in China
13/QED/1

ELIZABETH I

THE OUTCAST WHO BECAME ENGLAND'S QUEEN

· SIMON ADAMS

ELIZABETHA·MAGNA · · REGINA · ANGLIÆ ·

NATIONAL GEOGRAPHIC

WASHINGTON, D.C.

CONTENTS

BIRTH OF A PRINCESS

FROM PRISON TO THRONE

CONQUERING THE WORLD

GLORIOUS QUEEN

BIRTH OF A PRINCESS

I

A Royal Birth

On the afternoon of Sunday, September 7, 1533, sometime between 3 and 4 p.m., a baby girl was born in Greenwich, England. She was no ordinary baby, however, for her mother was Anne Boleyn, only recently crowned Queen of England, and her father was King Henry VIII, one of the most powerful monarchs in all Europe. One day, she too would become queen.

Three days later the baby was christened in a church next to the palace at Greenwich where she was born. As the christening took place, the watching soldiers and servants lit 500 torches and filled the church with light. The baby was named Elizabeth, the name of both her grandmothers. When the service was over, the Garter King of Arms, one of King Henry's main officials, made an announcement.

Previous page: This portrait of Elizabeth was probably painted in 1546 when she was just 13. It is the earliest known portrait of Elizabeth and is believed to have been painted for Henry VIII.

Left: Elizabeth's mother, Anne Boleyn, was of medium height, with dark brown hair and eyes. She was a clever and well-educated woman.

1485
Henry Tudor defeats Richard III in battle to seize the throne as Henry VII, the first Tudor king.

April 22, 1509
After the death of Henry VII, his son becomes king as Henry VIII.

Right: Elizabeth was christened in this fine dress of embroidered silk and lace, and wrapped in a long robe of purple velvet trimmed with ermine fur.

"God, of his infinite goodness, send prosperous life and long [life] to the high and mighty Princess of England, Elizabeth!" he called. A fanfare of trumpets filled the church.

After such a splendid ceremony, you would expect both mother and father to be delighted with their new child. But Anne had produced a princess for her king and Henry desperately wanted a boy. He already had one daughter, Mary, but he wanted a son to inherit the throne from him when he died. He had ended his marriage to his first wife, Katherine of Aragon, because she had not borne him a son, and now Anne Boleyn had failed him too.

When the christening was over, Elizabeth was taken back to the palace and placed in a specially prepared nursery. Screens protected her from any drafts, and every comfort was provided to make sure she was kept healthy and warm. She was watched over as she grew and learned to walk. But this peaceful childhood would not continue for long.

Boy or girl?

Before Elizabeth was born, letters were prepared to be sent out. The letters announced the birth and thanked God for sending the queen "good speed in the deliverance and bringing forth of a prince." An "s" had to be added to the word "prince" when it was clear the child was a girl. In Tudor times the word "princess" could be spelled with only one "s."

June 11, 1509
Henry VIII marries his brother's widow, Katherine of Aragon.

February 18, 1516
Mary, Elizabeth's older sister, is born to Katherine of Aragon.

The Tudors

Princess Elizabeth was born into a royal family known as the Tudors. The Tudors were Welsh in origin and did not have a strong claim to the throne. But in 1485, Elizabeth's grandfather, Henry Tudor, defeated and killed King Richard III in battle at Bosworth Field in Leicestershire. Henry then seized the throne to become the first Tudor king as Henry VII.

Richard III was a member of the royal house of York. Henry represented the rival house of Lancaster. These two royal houses had fought a civil war for the throne that lasted for 30 years. When Henry became king and ended the war, he married Elizabeth of York, the niece of Richard III, uniting the two houses. The Yorks had a white rose as their symbol; the Lancasters a red rose. Henry put the colors together as the Tudor rose.

Henry VII ruled for 24 years until his death in 1509. His eldest son, Arthur, had died in 1502, so his second son, Henry, became king as Henry VIII. The new king's first wife was Arthur's widow, Katherine of Aragon, a Spanish princess.

Left: The red and white Tudor Rose, symbol of Elizabeth's Tudor family, combined the roses of two former royal houses united in marriage by Elizabeth's grandfather, Henry Tudor.

1527
Henry VIII asks the pope to annul his marriage to Katherine, but is refused.

January 1533
Henry VIII marries Lady Anne Boleyn.

She bore him a daughter, Mary, in 1516. In 1525, Henry fell in love with Anne Boleyn. He annulled, or canceled, his marriage to Katherine to marry Anne, who gave birth to Elizabeth.

Henry still wanted a son, so in 1536 he executed Anne on charges of adultery and married Jane Seymour, one of her ladies-in-waiting. The next year, Jane produced the son and heir, Edward, that Henry wanted. But Jane died only 12 days after Edward's birth. In January 1540, Henry married a fourth time. Anne of Cleves was a German princess, but Henry found her ugly and the marriage was swiftly ended. That same July, he married his fifth wife, Katherine Howard, but executed her in 1542 for having several lovers. His sixth and final wife was Katherine Parr, whom he married in 1543. When Henry died in 1547, he was succeeded by his son Edward, who had no children. When Edward died, his elder sister Mary became queen.

Below: In this painting of the Tudor family, Henry VIII is shown with his third wife, Jane Seymour, to his left, and his three children: Mary to his far left, Edward, to his right, and Elizabeth to his far right.

July 1533
Henry VIII is excommunicated from the Catholic Church for annulling his marriage to Katherine.

September 7, 1533
Elizabeth is born at Greenwich Palace, southeast of London. She is the child of Anne Boleyn and Henry VIII.

The Tudor Kingdom

The kingdom ruled by the Tudors was not the one their successors rule today. England conquered Wales, a neighboring country, in 1284, but the two were not united until the Act of Union in 1536, three years after Elizabeth was born. Ireland had been under English rule since 1171. In 1541, Henry VIII gave himself the title King of Ireland. Scotland meanwhile, was a totally independent nation ruled over by the Stewart (later Stuart) dynasty. This was despite almost constant attempts by English kings to conquer the country.

ELIZABETH'S FAMILY TREE

HENRY VII
RULED 1485–1509

- **ARTHUR**
- **HENRY VIII**
  RULED 1509–1547
- **MARGARET**
- **MARY**

- **MARY I**
  RULED 1553–1558
- **ELIZABETH I**
  RULED 1558–1603
- **EDWARD VI**
  RULED 1547–1553
- **JAMES V OF SCOTLAND**
- **FRANCES**

- **MARY QUEEN OF SCOTS**
- **LADY JANE GREY**

- **JAMES I (VI OF SCOTLAND)**
  RULED 1603–1625

Above: The Tudor Rose (top) was the symbol of the five Tudor monarchs, starting with Henry VII in 1485 and ending with Elizabeth herself, who reigned from 1558.

Below: Tudor England was governed from Westminster, just to the west of the City of London. Parliament met in St. Stephen's Chapel (on the left), and the law courts were held in Westminster Hall (center). Westminster Abbey is on the right.

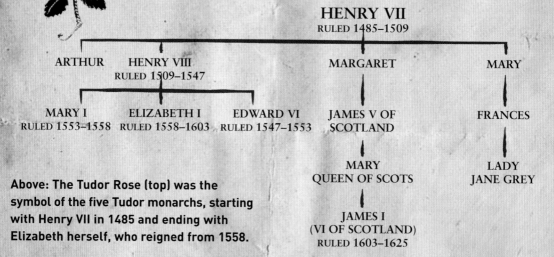

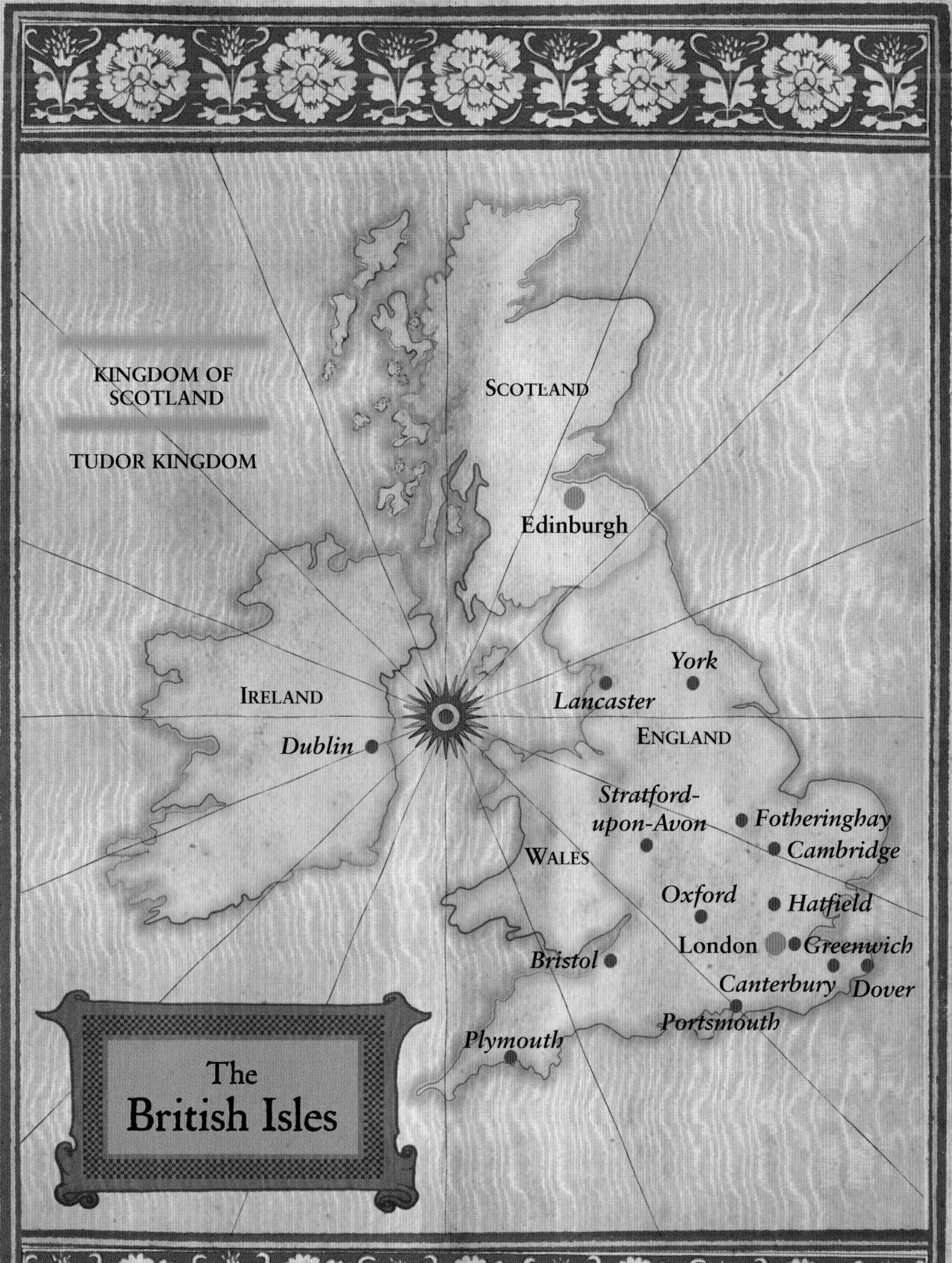

KINGDOM OF
SCOTLAND

TUDOR KINGDOM

SCOTLAND

Edinburgh

York

Lancaster

IRELAND

ENGLAND

Dublin

Stratford-
upon-Avon

Fotheringhay

Cambridge

WALES

Oxford

Hatfield

London

Greenwich

Bristol

Canterbury

Dover

Portsmouth

Plymouth

The
British Isles

Elizabeth's Early Life

When Elizabeth was about six months old, Henry began negotiations for her to marry a French prince. By annulling his first marriage, he had made Elizabeth heir to the throne in place of her older half-sister, Mary. Elizabeth's future looked happy and secure. But all this changed in 1536 when her mother was executed. From then on, Elizabeth's life was filled with danger.

After the birth of Elizabeth, Henry still longed for a son, but Anne failed to produce any more children. Henry soon lost interest in Anne and accused her of being an unfaithful wife. She was taken to the Tower of London, the fortress used to imprison important people. There, on May 15, she was put on trial. Because she was queen, the charge was high treason, in other words that she had betrayed the king of the country. Anne was found guilty and, after her marriage to Henry was declared invalid, she was executed on May 19. Elizabeth was not even three years old.

In all her life, Elizabeth is known to have talked about her mother only twice.

Left: This portrait of Lord Cobham and his family, probably painted during the 1550s, gives a good idea of the sort of mealtimes Elizabeth and her friends enjoyed together.

1534
Henry VIII makes himself head of the English church.

May 19, 1536
Elizabeth's mother, Anne Boleyn, is executed for high treason.

> *"I have dealt with many learned ladies, but amongst them all the brightest star is my illustrious Lady Elizabeth."*
>
> **Roger Ascham, tutor to Elizabeth**

But it is known that her life changed dramatically for the worse the day her mother died. Within days of her mother's death, Elizabeth was declared illegitimate and so was no longer in line for the throne.

Elizabeth was cared for first by Lady Margaret Bryan and then, starting at the age of four, by Katherine Champernowne, known as Kat. Kat soon became devoted to Elizabeth. Tutors taught Elizabeth mathematics, astronomy, history, geography, architecture, needlework, horseback riding, and dancing. She was also taught Latin, and by the age of ten was learning French, Italian, and Greek. She was an intelligent girl who enjoyed her lessons.

Below: Like these young children, Elizabeth would have played with rattles and hobby horses, as well as playing catch with cushions.

1536–1539
All the Catholic monasteries and priories in England are closed down as Henry seizes their wealth.

October 12, 1537
Prince Edward, later Edward VI, is born to Henry VIII and his third wife, Jane Seymour.

Left: Katherine Parr, Henry VIII's sixth wife, had already been married and widowed twice before she married Henry in 1543. After his death in 1547, she married for a fourth time, to Thomas Seymour.

The relationship between Elizabeth and Kat became even closer in 1545, when Kat married John Ashley, a cousin of Elizabeth's mother.

Elizabeth lived in four different royal houses north of London, moving between them from month to month. She sometimes saw her brother and sister. She did not see her father much, but he sent messengers to ask about her health and education.

In 1543, Elizabeth's life changed for the better when her father married for the sixth and final time. His new wife, Katherine Parr, was an intelligent, educated woman who got on well with her three stepchildren. She encouraged Henry to see more of his two daughters, both of whom he eventually reinstated as his heirs after Edward. Elizabeth got along very well with her young brother, but as she grew older, her relationship with her sister Mary grew worse. Mary blamed Elizabeth's mother Anne Boleyn for all her own misfortunes and suffering, and transferred that blame to Elizabeth.

Making fun

Although Elizabeth was good at learning languages, her spoken French was not that good. The French ambassador used to mimic her accent, for she made all her "A" sounds faaaaar too long!

January 6, 1540	July 9, 1540
Henry VIII marries his fourth wife, Anne of Cleves.	The marriage to Anne of Cleves is annulled.

Right: Elizabeth's younger half-brother, Prince Edward, was only four years younger than she was, and she was very fond of him. When he became king in 1547, the two remained friends.

Elizabeth gradually became more independent. She spoke and wrote Greek and Latin fluently, and had mastered Italian, Spanish, and even a little Welsh, the language of her Tudor ancestors. She was also becoming an attractive young woman.

In 1547, Henry VIII died and was succeeded by his nine-year-old son, Edward. Almost immediately, the 13-year-old Elizabeth was engulfed in scandal. The new king's uncle, Lord Thomas Seymour, wanted to increase his own power by marrying Elizabeth. When he realized that this would be impossible because of opposition from other nobles, he married her stepmother, Katherine Parr. Thomas moved into Hatfield Palace and began to make advances toward Elizabeth, attempting to kiss her. Katherine stopped him and, in May 1548, Elizabeth was sent away to the countryside. After Katherine's death that September, Thomas again tried to marry Elizabeth. In January 1549, he was arrested and charged with treason against Edward.

Elizabeth was questioned about her relationship with Seymour. When Seymour was executed in March 1549, Elizabeth's life too was under threat, but she continued to deny any wrongdoing. Eventually, her story was believed and she returned to Hatfield to continue her education.

July 28, 1540
Henry VIII marries Katherine Howard, but has her beheaded two years later for treason and adultery.

December 6 or 7, 1542
Mary, future Queen of Scots, is born at Linlithgow Palace, Scotland. She is Elizabeth's second cousin.

Daily Life in Tudor Times

The world into which Elizabeth was born and where she grew up was very different from the world of today. It was a much harsher place, where people lived far shorter lives and often suffered great hardship and poverty.

The population of England and Wales at the start of the Tudor period was about 2.3 million, rising to about 3 million people when Elizabeth was growing up. Compared with the present population of 52 million, England was much emptier than it is today. Most people lived in country towns or in the countryside. There were no large cities and only a few big towns.

Medicine was primitive and medical knowledge limited, so illness and death were frequent events in most households. If they lived through infancy—and most babies did not—children would have had to survive frequent outbreaks of plague and smallpox.

Left: Tudor teachers believed pain was good for their students, so many whipped them with canes, bundles of birch twigs, or leather straps.

1543
Henry VIII marries Katherine Parr, his sixth and final wife.

1544
Elizabeth is reinstated as a legitimate heir to the throne, after Edward and Mary.

Below: The Tudor kitchen was a place to cook, eat, and socialize. Every kitchen had a large open fire on which to cook, roast, and boil the food.

There were three main classes, or groups of people, in Tudor England. The smallest and richest class—of which Elizabeth was a member—was the nobility, those people with hereditary titles, such as dukes and earls, including the royal family itself. Below them was a larger and growing class of professional people, such as lawyers and merchants. The lowest class was the large working group of farm workers, craftspeople, laborers, servants, and other poor people.

Growing up fast

Tudor children became adults much faster than children do today. Boys could get married at 14, whereas girls only had to wait until they were 12.

Only rich boys, and a few rich girls like Elizabeth, received an education. Girls were taught by tutors at home, whereas rich boys went to grammar school or were taught by tutors. Only a few boys went to university.

January 1547

Henry VIII dies. His son becomes king as Edward VI.

April 1547

Henry's widow, Katherine Parr, marries the new king's uncle, Thomas Seymour.

Poor boys received no education or just a very basic one in the local village or town. They then went out to work the land, or became servants or apprentices to local craftspeople.

Most people lived off the land, growing wheat, barley, vegetables, and fruit. They kept hens and ducks, caught fish from the rivers and lakes, and hunted rabbits, wildfowl, and other game. They used honey to sweeten their food, as they had no sugar. Food was preserved and seasoned with herbs and salt, but spices were rare, as they came from abroad.

Many of the great banquets the young Elizabeth attended at court were extraordinary feasts. Some of the dishes were particularly scrumptious.

Below: Weddings were a great cause for celebration, as this painting of a wedding in Bermondsey, now part of south London, shows. Guests contributed food and drink and brought their own instruments to accompany the dancers.

September 10, 1547
English forces defeat the Scots at the Battle of Pinkie.

1547–1553
Boys' schools are established in many small towns during the reign of Edward VI.

There was peacock stuffed with dried fruit and spices; baked porpoise pie; roast blackbird; and for dessert, a mixture of ground almonds, honey, and rose water made into the shape of a castle, a flower, or an animal. After a royal feast had ended, the servants cleared away the leftover food and ate what they wanted. The rest was given to the poor, who crowded around the palace gates.

Above: Soccer was often played in the open fields and meadows. There was no limit to how many men and women could play for each team.

English people enjoyed a wide range of entertainments. Rich people jousted on horses or hunted for deer and other wild animals. They played bowls or tennis, or stayed indoors to play chess or a board game, or perhaps a musical instrument. As a young girl, Elizabeth learned to play the harpsichord and other stringed instruments such as the lute.

Poor people made up their own entertainments. Then, as now, soccer was a popular sport. The goalposts could be up to two or three miles apart on either side of a town or large meadow.

Eating all night

Elizabeth's father, Henry VIII, loved to eat and drink. He once gave a banquet for the German ambassador that started at 7 p.m. and did not finish until two o'clock the next morning, seven hours later. The guests were served ten courses, including fish pies that looked like castles and meats of every type.

1549
Elizabeth is engulfed in scandal about her relationship with Thomas Seymour.

January 1549
An Act of Parliament demands that all English churches use a Protestant prayer book.

Catholics and Protestants

When Elizabeth was born in 1533, England was in the middle of a huge religious argument. At the center of this argument was Henry's marriage to Elizabeth's mother, an event that had split the church. During Elizabeth's childhood and early adulthood, there were rebellions that left many people dead.

Above: By 1540, every monastery, abbey, friary, priory, and nunnery in the country had been closed, including the massive Fountains Abbey in Yorkshire.

Henry VIII was born and brought up a Catholic. The Catholic Church was led by the pope in Rome and was the only church in the whole of western Europe.

The Catholic Church had become very rich and corrupt. In 1517, a German monk, Martin Luther, objected to this corruption, and began a movement now called the Reformation. This Protestant movement set up churches throughout northern Europe. Henry argued strongly against Luther. So grateful was the pope for Henry's support that, in 1521, he gave him the title *Fidei Defensor*—"Defender of the Faith." This is a title the queen of England still bears today, and the Latin initials "FD" are on British coins.

August 1549

After a brief period of peace, war is renewed between England and France.

1550

The population of England has slowly grown to about three million people.

> *"The king's majesty justly and rightfully is and ought to be the supreme head of the Church of England."*
>
> **From the 1534 Act of Supremacy recognizing Henry VIII as head of the English church**

Without a divorce from his first wife, Katherine, Henry could not marry Anne Boleyn. When the pope refused to grant him a divorce, because it was against the rules of the Catholic church, Henry got the marriage annulled anyway and married Anne. The pope answered by excommunicating Henry. Henry made himself supreme head of the English church in place of the pope.

Rebellions broke out across England and many people were executed for opposing the king. Elizabeth, however, had known no other religion and accepted the beliefs of the new church. As she grew up, there were more reforms. For the first time ever, people attended church services held in English, not Latin, and the Bible was published in English so that everyone could read it.

By the 1550s, it looked as if all this religious argument was dying down. But in 1553, Edward VI died at age 15, and the throne passed to his eldest sister, Mary. She was a Catholic.

Above: Elizabeth remained true to the new religion that spread through England in the 1530s, but she was not extreme in her own beliefs.

FROM PRISON TO
THRONE

Sent to the Tower

The short reign of Elizabeth's sister, Mary, was a time of great danger for Elizabeth. Her life was often under threat, and it seemed possible that she would end her days as her mother did, executed in the Tower of London. Yet she survived, emerging from it a strong and determined young woman.

Elizabeth's troubles began at the very end of her brother Edward's reign. He was persuaded by his powerful advisers to make his cousin, Lady Jane Grey, heir to the throne to stop Mary and Elizabeth becoming queen. This was because Lady Jane Grey was a Protestant, unlike Mary, who was Catholic. Jane becoming queen would make sure the Protestant reforms of Edward's reign would remain after his death. When Edward died in July 1553, Lady Jane was proclaimed queen. Mary rallied public support and within nine days had seized the throne, imprisoning Lady Jane in the Tower of London.

Previous page: This small portrait of Elizabeth was painted sometime during the 1550s, before she became queen in 1558.

Left: Painted in 1544 when she was 28 and not yet queen, this portrait of Mary by Master John shows her looking severe and sad.

July 1553
Edward VI dies and is succeeded first briefly by a cousin, Lady Jane Grey, and then by Mary, his sister.

January 1554
Sir Thomas Wyatt leads a rebellion against Mary's proposed marriage to Philip II of Spain.

Right: On Palm Sunday, March 18, 1554, Elizabeth was carried by barge down the River Thames and into the Tower of London through Traitor's Gate.

As soon as Mary became queen, she began to reinstate Catholicism as the official religion. She also had Protestants who refused to convert to Catholicism burned at the stake.

In late 1553, Mary announced her intention to marry Philip II, Catholic king of Spain. As a result, a rebellion, led by Sir Thomas Wyatt, marched on London, but the revolt was easily crushed. Mary believed that Elizabeth was involved. On March 18, 1554, Elizabeth was sent to the Tower of London. She wrote to her sister to try to convince Mary that she was innocent, but Mary would not release her.

Elizabeth remained in the Tower until mid-May, but she continued to say she was innocent and nothing could be proved against her. In the end, she was released to Woodstock Palace in Oxfordshire, where she was kept under house arrest. She stayed there until October 1555, when she was allowed to return to her house in Hatfield, although she was still kept under constant supervision.

Prison graffiti

When Elizabeth was held under house arrest at Woodstock Palace in 1554, she allegedly used her diamond ring to scratch onto a windowpane the following words:
"Much suspected of me,
Nothing proved can be,
Quoth Elizabeth, prisoner."

March 18, 1554
Elizabeth is imprisoned in the Tower on suspicion of involvement in Wyatt's rebellion.

May 19, 1554
Elizabeth is released from the Tower.

Becoming Queen

Mary's marriage to Philip of Spain was not a success, and she had no children. She had not managed to get rid of the Protestant religion, and the English were hungry after years of bad harvests. The French had won back Calais, on the French coast, which had been in English hands for over 200 years. Worn out and disappointed, Mary died in November 1558. Her heir was Elizabeth.

At this time, Elizabeth was living in Hatfield Palace. Two members of the Privy Council came to Hatfield to tell her the news just before noon.

Elizabeth was sitting under an oak tree, reading the New Testament of the Bible in Greek. As she stood up to greet her guests, they knelt down in front of her and saluted her as queen of England. Elizabeth was overcome for a minute and then composed herself and fell to her knees in prayer, speaking the words of the 118th Psalm.

Left: Elizabeth in her coronation robes wears a beautiful gold crown set with rubies, diamonds, and pearls. She holds the royal orb and scepter in her hands.

July 25, 1554
Mary marries Philip II of Spain in Winchester Cathedral.

1557
In support of her Spanish husband, Mary declares war on France.

> *"This is the Lord's doing: it is marvelous in our eyes!"*
> **Elizabeth I quoting the 118th Psalm on hearing news of becoming queen**

Elizabeth was just 25, and her life of imprisonment and rejection was now over. She was Queen of England and had work to do. She chose William Cecil as her chief minister and selected a small council of ministers to advise her. She left Hatfield and went first to the Charterhouse in London before taking up residence in Whitehall Palace, the main royal palace in London, to prepare for her coronation.

On Thursday, January 12, 1559, Elizabeth went down the River Thames in a barge to stay in the Tower of London, which was a royal palace as well as a prison. Two days later, she made a triumphant procession through the City of London. The streets were lined with banners and flags, crowds cheering their new queen, and musicians and actors performing little pageants on specially built stages along the route. The queen listened attentively to every speech and even spoke to people in the crowd. The next day, Sunday, January 15, Elizabeth was crowned queen in Westminster Abbey. The abbey had been the traditional setting for coronations since William the Conqueror was crowned king there in 1066.

Royal robes
For her coronation, Elizabeth wore the same robes her sister, Mary, had worn in 1553, although with newly made sleeves and a bodice to fit her. The dress was typical of a fine Tudor dress of the period, with a narrow waist, a flowing skirt, and a ruff around the neck.

November 17, 1558
Mary I dies in London. Elizabeth becomes queen.

November 23, 1558
Elizabeth leaves Hatfield for the Charterhouse in London.

The Young Ruler

As queen, Elizabeth faced enormous problems. Through Mary's marriage, England was allied with Catholic Spain, yet Elizabeth was head of a new church. England had just lost its last territory on the European mainland to France and had suffered years of religious turmoil. Elizabeth overcame these and many other problems, and became a very successful monarch.

Above: Elizabeth dances the lively galliard at court with her favorite, Robert Dudley. Men were advised to remove their swords for this dance for safety reasons.

At age 25, Elizabeth was of average height and slender build, with the same red hair and slightly hooked nose as her father. She inherited her mother's long, thin face, pointed chin, and dark eyes. Her skin was pale and her eyelashes and eyebrows so pale that they were almost nonexistent. Her hands were thin and white, with long fingers. She was not beautiful, although the ambassador from Venice, Italy, described her as "very handsome." And everyone commented on her regal behavior.

November 1558
Elizabeth appoints William Cecil her principal secretary. Together they pick a small Privy Council to advise her.

1558 onward
Elizabeth continues her sister Mary's alliance with Spain to counteract the threat from France.

Musical talent

Elizabeth was a fine musician and played the lute and harpsichord, both to entertain her friends and also simply for herself, to "shun [drive away] melancholy."

Elizabeth was clever at handling people and events. She was highly intelligent and hardworking. Never a day went by when she did not read a book or write a letter. She was also an excellent judge of people.

However, her childhood experiences made her distrustful and wary in her dealings with them. Temperamental and quick-tempered, she could be very sharp when irritated, and sometimes very sarcastic and cutting. She was also extraordinarily vain—another thing she had inherited from her mother—and loved the attention and compliments paid to her by her courtiers. She erupted into outbursts of rage, which quickly subsided. As a child, she had suffered panic attacks that almost paralyzed her.

Elizabeth's greatest quality was her character. She had a strong personality and genuine charm, and this earned her everyone's respect. Her vitality and love of life she inherited from her father, Henry VIII. She was very witty; loved to dance, listen to and play music; and she enjoyed horseback riding, hunting, and other outdoor pursuits. After the serious days of Mary's reign, Elizabeth brought excitement and fun back into the court and the country.

Marked for life

In 1562, Elizabeth suffered a bout of smallpox that left her face pockmarked and scarred. From then on, she covered these marks with elaborate makeup to appear as young and beautiful as possible.

January 14, 1559
Elizabeth makes a triumphant procession through the City of London.

January 15, 1559
Elizabeth is crowned queen in Westminster Abbey.

Elizabeth's Suitors

Elizabeth would have been a wonderful catch for any man. She was attractive, witty, and highly intelligent. And she was queen. Many men offered to marry her. Elizabeth enjoyed the flattery and attention, but maybe never had any intention of marrying. One observer remarked, "The Queen would like everyone to be in love with her, but I doubt whether she will ever be in love with anyone enough to marry them." She herself said in April 1558, just seven months before she became queen, that she wished "to remain in that estate that I was [unmarried], which of all others best liked me."

Left: Lord Robert Dudley, later Earl of Leicester, was one of Elizabeth's suitors. Because of the suspicious death of his first wife in 1560, and opposition from other noblemen, the two remained only close friends until his death in 1588.

WHY DID SHE NEVER MARRY?

Elizabeth needed to marry to produce an heir to the throne. Her main problem was that if she married a foreign king or nobleman, England might fall under foreign rule and she did not want that. However, if she married an Englishman, she would be marrying beneath her royal status. Either candidate would meet with opposition, and this is one reason why she never married.

Right: Robert Devereux, Earl of Essex, the stepson of Robert Dudley, was 33 years younger than Elizabeth. Despite the age difference, he became a firm favorite until he rebelled against Elizabeth's government. He was executed for treason in 1601.

FOREIGN PRINCES

One of the earliest offers of marriage Elizabeth received was in January 1559, from Philip II of Spain, the widower of her sister, Mary. Elizabeth refused him. She refused at least a dozen other foreign princes, including Duke Eric of Finland, Archdukes Ferdinand and Charles of Austria, and the dukes of Holstein and Saxony in Germany.

The one foreign prince who came close to marrying Elizabeth was Francis, Duke of Anjou, the brother of Henry III of France. He was 21 years younger than she, but the marriage would have made strong the alliance of England and France against Spain. Many in England objected. Negotiations to arrange the marriage were dragged out for five years until the duke died in 1584.

Governing the Country

The main problem Elizabeth faced as queen was that she was a young woman in a world in which men held all the powerful positions in both the government and the church. She had to use all her intellect and personal strengths to rule the country, but needed help to do it well.

When Mary was queen, she had a large Privy Council to advise her on domestic and foreign policy. Some of them were Protestant, others Catholic; some were pro-French, others pro-Spanish. As a result, Mary often got conflicting or bad advice. When she became queen, Elizabeth chose her council of only 19 men. She considered that it was better to have only a few people who gave good advice. She placed absolute trust in her council. In return, she demanded total loyalty and plain speaking. Most of them were members of her own family, or friends and relatives of her chief minister, William Cecil. Cecil had served as principal secretary to Edward VI from 1550 but then lost his power when Mary became queen.

Left: Elizabeth wrote in a fine script, signing her name with magnificent loops and other flourishes of the pen.

January 1559
Elizabeth announces her new policies to Parliament.

Easter 1559
Elizabeth first washes the feet of the poor at the Maundy Thursday service, a royal ritual still carried out today.

Left: When Elizabeth addressed Parliament, she sat on a throne high above the chamber in the House of Lords. Members of the House of Commons stood at the far end.

Elizabeth made him her main adviser and her principal secretary—her chief minister—when she became queen. In 1571, she gave him the title Baron Burghley, and he continued to serve her faithfully until his death in 1598. Elizabeth trusted him totally: "This judgement I have of you, that you will not be corrupted with any manner of gift...and that without respect of my private will, you will give me that counsel that you think best."

The laws of England were discussed and approved in Parliament, which met in Westminster. The House of Commons—the lower house of Parliament—consisted of members elected from across the country, and Elizabeth always treated it with great respect. She regularly addressed Parliament and took great care in writing her own speeches. The members of Parliament returned this respect, and Elizabeth never lost their support.

Spying for the queen

Elizabeth's spymaster, Sir Francis Walsingham, employed a large number of spies to find information about Elizabeth's enemies at home and abroad. They got information by stealing and opening private letters, breaking secret codes, and torturing suspects.

May 1559
The Act of Supremacy reinstates the Protestant faith. Elizabeth is Supreme Governor of the Church of England.

1561
After the death of her husband, Francis II of France, Mary Queen of Scots returns to Scotland.

Life at Court

At the center of Elizabeth's life was the royal court, presided over by Elizabeth herself. The court consisted of officers of the royal household, members of the Privy Council, and the queen's own private staff. It was the center of royal power, but also a place of entertainment.

The size of the royal court varied from year to year. When Elizabeth was in residence in one of her larger palaces, such as Hampton Court or Whitehall, it could number up to 1,500 people, including cooks, gardeners, and other servants. Rules to organize this vast number of people were first laid down by Elizabeth's great-grandfather Edward IV in the 1460s. These rules covered every aspect of court life.

One of the most important things covered by the rules was the supply of food. Strict order was vital due to the huge quantity of food eaten: records show that in 1591 Elizabeth's court ate 1,240 oxen, 8,200 sheep, 2,330 deer, 1,870 pigs, 53 wild boar, and more than 40 million eggs. All this happened at a time when there was no canned food or refrigerators to store fresh produce. The monarch had the right to buy this food from local farmers and merchants at well below its usual cost.

Giving presents

At New Year, Elizabeth and her court exchanged gifts, just as a family does at Christmas today. Elizabeth received jewelry, handkerchiefs, sweets, and pastries, in return for which she gave plates made of gold.

1562
Elizabeth almost dies of smallpox, but eventually recovers, to great public rejoicing.

1563
The beliefs of the Church of England are set out in the 39 Articles of Religion.

Maids in waiting

Elizabeth was helped by up to six unpaid maids of honor—usually young, unmarried women of high birth—who waited on her at court. She also employed seven or eight gentlewomen, four chambermaids, and four ladies of the bedchamber.

The rules also controlled the elaborate rituals designed to show off the power and importance of Elizabeth as queen. Every court event, whether it was a procession through the streets of London; a royal banquet; a christening, wedding, or funeral; or the exchange of gifts at New Year, had strict rules. These ranked everyone according to their title, gender, and order of birth.

During the summer months, the court went on tour around the country, staying in the stately homes of the great landowners. Elizabeth never traveled light—some 200 to 300 carts went with her carrying everything from her clothes to state documents. The cost of this travel was immense, as the tour could last up to 12 weeks. Entertainments such as plays, balls, and tournaments were held at every house, while Elizabeth and her courtiers could also enjoy country pursuits such as hunting, riding horses, and hawking.

Right: One of Elizabeth's most important duties was to meet foreign officials at court. Here she greets two ambassadors from Holland in London in 1585.

1563
A quarter of London's population dies of the plague.

1565
Mary Queen of Scots marries her cousin, Lord Darnley.

CONQUERING
THE WORLD

European Rivals

Although Elizabeth ruled over a largely peaceful nation, she faced problems abroad. Throughout her reign, Europe endured wars and conflicts that split the continent and nearly threatened the independence of England itself.

The main power in Europe was the Habsburg family, originally from Austria. During the reign of Emperor Charles V (1516–1556), the Habsburgs controlled Austria, Hungary, much of Germany and Italy, the Netherlands (now the Netherlands and Belgium), Spain, and all Spain's vast colonies in South and Central America. In 1556, Charles V abdicated and split his empire in two. The eastern half went to his brother Ferdinand. The western half, including Spain, went to his son Philip II.

Previous page: The English fleet engages the Spanish Armada in battle in the English Channel in July 1588.

Left: Philip II of Spain was the most powerful ruler in Europe and a constant threat to Elizabeth and England.

1566

A son, the future James I, is born to Elizabeth's cousin, Mary Queen of Scots.

1568

After abdicating her throne, Mary Queen of Scots flees to England, where she is imprisoned.

Europe was also split by religion. The Reformation had divided Europe into Catholic and Protestant nations. England was the leading Protestant power in Europe, and Spain and France the leading Catholic nations. Elizabeth tried to stop Spain and France from invading England to restore the Catholic faith. She also tried to prevent France from allying with England's oldest enemy, Scotland. Her cousin Mary Queen of Scots had as good a claim to the English throne as Elizabeth, and Mary was a Catholic.

In 1570, the pope excommunicated Elizabeth because she was a Protestant, just as he had done her father in 1533. This led Philip II of Spain to plot against Elizabeth. In response, Elizabeth began to support the Dutch rebels who were fighting for independence from Spain. This was a way to weaken Spanish power in Europe and prevent the Spanish from using the Netherlands as a base from which to attack England. In 1587, this juggling act came to an end when Elizabeth was forced to deal with her cousin Mary Queen of Scots.

Living forever?

Philip II of Spain controlled a vast empire in both Europe and the Americas but he insisted on making every decision himself. He had so much work to do and was so far behind doing it that people used to joke that, if death came from Spain, everyone would be immortal.

No winners

When Elizabeth was excommunicated by Pope Pius V in February 1570, English Catholics were placed in a very difficult position. If they continued to support their queen, they too would be excommunicated, but if they supported the pope, they risked charges of treason.

1570
The pope excommunicates Elizabeth.

1571
Philip II of Spain becomes more hostile, and Elizabeth moves closer to France.

Mary Queen of Scots

In 1568, Elizabeth received a most unwelcome visitor. Her cousin Mary Queen of Scots had been forced to leave Scotland after losing her crown. For the next 19 years, Mary became the greatest problem that Elizabeth had to face, for she was both a rival for Elizabeth's own throne and a Catholic.

Mary had been Queen of Scotland since she was six days old, after her father James V was killed in battle by Henry VIII in 1542. Her grandmother was Margaret Tudor, older sister of Henry VIII. Mary was raised a Catholic, and many Catholics wanted her to be Queen of England. Mary had the right to inherit the throne if Elizabeth had no children. Mary had strong allies because she had lived in France from the age of five. She had also married the heir to the French throne. When her husband Francis briefly became king in 1559, Mary was Queen of Scotland and France.

Left: Nicholas Hilliard's portrait of Elizabeth is known as the Pelican Portrait because of the queen's brooch. The pelican represented charity and self-sacrifice.

1584
An expedition to southeast North America names the area Virginia after Elizabeth, the Virgin Queen.

1585
Elizabeth sends an army under the Earl of Leicester to help Dutch rebels fight for independence from Spain.

After her husband's death, Mary returned to Scotland in 1561, and in 1565 married her cousin Lord Darnley. The marriage was never happy, and a jealous Darnley had Mary's close friend and secretary, David Rizzio, murdered in front of her in March 1566. Less than a year later, Darnley was killed and Mary married his probable murderer, the Earl of Bothwell. The Scottish nobles forced her to abdicate, and she fled to England in May 1568.

While in England, Mary was arrested and held in various castles. She plotted frequently against Elizabeth, and in 1586 was involved in a plot by Sir Thomas Babington to assassinate Elizabeth. Mary was transferred to Fotheringhay Castle in Northamptonshire and put on trial for treason.

On October 25, 1586, Mary was found guilty and sentenced to death. Elizabeth was extremely reluctant to sign the death warrant, and only did so on February 1, 1587. Seven days later, Mary was executed, causing outrage across Catholic Europe.

Right: Like her cousin Elizabeth, Mary Queen of Scots was highly intelligent, but also very hot-tempered and proud. She made many enemies during her life.

February 1587
Mary Queen of Scots is executed for plotting against Elizabeth.

April 1587
The English captain Sir Francis Drake attacks Cadiz in Spain.

Explorers and Seafarers

SIR FRANCIS DRAKE

Francis Drake was born into a seafaring family in Devon, England, around 1542. He made his reputation seizing gold and silver from Spanish treasure ships crossing the Atlantic on their way home from the New World to Spain. In 1577, Drake left Plymouth, England, on board the *Pelican* (above, later renamed the *Golden Hind*), with four other ships. He sailed counter-clockwise around the world, attacking Spanish treasure ships in the Pacific Ocean and trading in expensive spices and other goods. He returned home in 1581, the first Englishman to circumnavigate the globe. After a massive banquet on board ship, Elizabeth knighted him. Drake played a major role in the defeat of the Armada and died in the Caribbean in 1596.

WALTER RALEIGH

In 1584, Walter Raleigh set out across the Atlantic Ocean to explore the coast of North America. He wanted to find out if it was a suitable place to create England's first colony overseas. The following year he set sail again, this time settling 107 people on Roanoke Island off the coast of Virginia. Among those on board was John White, who recorded the expedition and drew the Native American town of Pomeiock (above). The settlement was not a success because it depended on trading with local people. A second attempt was made in 1587, but when Raleigh returned in 1590, he found no trace of the settlers. However, the two attempts did pave the way for the establishment of England's first successful colony, in Jamestown, Virginia, in 1607.

The Spanish Armada

In the summer of 1588, Elizabeth faced one of the greatest challenges of her reign. A huge armada from Spain threatened to invade the country and remove her from the throne. Her future, and the future of England, hung in the balance. But a combination of English seamanship and bad weather saved the day, giving Elizabeth one of the great naval victories of all time.

The execution of Mary Queen of Scots finally convinced Philip II of Spain that he must do all in his power to overthrow Elizabeth. Not only had she been aiding Dutch rebels in their fight against his rule, but her seamen had been raiding his treasure ships laden with gold and silver as they sailed back from the New World to Spain. Philip had been preparing an invasion fleet since 1585, even before Mary's death. But his plans were disrupted when, in April

1587, the English captain Sir Francis Drake sailed into Cadiz Harbor, Spain, and destroyed many Spanish ships at anchor. He described the attack as "singeing the King of Spain's beard."

Left: The English set fire to eight ships and sailed them into the Armada anchored off Calais, forcing the Spanish to leave their anchorage and head out to sea.

May 20, 1588
The Armada sets sail from Spanish-controlled Lisbon, in Portugal.

July 19, 1588
The Armada is sighted in the English Channel.

Philip was furious, but Drake had bought time for the English to get ships ready to defend themselves.

On May 20, 1588, the Armada, with more than 130 ships, set sail from Lisbon, the Portuguese capital held by Spain. Bad winds forced the fleet into La Coruna on the Spanish coast, where it took on supplies, before it crossed the Bay of Biscay into the English Channel. At 4 p.m. on July 19, the Armada was sighted off Lizard Point in Cornwall. As it sailed up the Channel, two of its ships were picked off by the English fleet. On July 27, the Armada anchored off Calais.

The Spanish plan was to use the Armada to protect the large invasion force of about 17,000 men—waiting in the Spanish Netherlands—as it crossed over in small ships to England. But that invasion force was not ready, so the English seized their chance. The next day, they set fire to eight of their own ships and sailed them into the Spanish fleet. The Spanish quickly upped anchor and sailed out into the English Channel, where a major battle took place off Gravelines, just northeast of Calais.

Above: The Armada set out from Lisbon and traveled up the English Channel before heading north around Scotland.

July 28, 1588
The English send in fireships to break up the Armada off Calais.

July 29, 1588
After the decisive encounter off Gravelines, the Armada sails up into the North Sea.

Using superior seamanship, better artillery, and more maneuverable ships, the English scattered the Armada, forcing it into the North Sea.

A few days later, the Spanish commander, the Duke of Medina Sidonia, decided that, if wind and weather allowed, the Armada would turn around and head back to Calais. But if the wind continued to blow from the southwest, the Armada should continue northward, up the North Sea, around the top of Scotland and Ireland, and then south to Spain.

Below: The "Armada" portrait was painted to celebrate Elizabeth's victory. She rests her hand on the globe—a symbol of her international power—and stands in front of paintings of the defeated, wrecked Armada and the victorious English fleet.

August 2, 1588
The Duke of Medina Sidonia orders the Armada to sail home around the top of Scotland and Ireland.

August 8, 1588
Elizabeth makes a famous address to her troops at Tilbury, Essex.

> *"I know I have the body but of a weak and feeble woman, but I have the heart and stomach of a king, and of a king of England too."*
>
> **Elizabeth rallying her troops at Tilbury, August 8, 1588**

The wind did not change direction, so the Armada sailed northward, where it was slowly defeated, not by the pursuing English ships but by autumn gales. Numerous ships were wrecked on the rocky Scottish and Irish coasts, and hundreds of sailors were killed by local people as they staggered ashore from the wrecks. By the time the fleet struggled into La Coruna that winter, only half its ships and men had made it safely home.

Elizabeth had already made a stirring speech to English soldiers waiting at Tilbury, Essex, about defending London from attack. When it became clear that the Armada had been defeated, England erupted in celebration. People lit bonfires and rang church bells. In London, Elizabeth processed through the streets to a thanksgiving service in St. Paul's Cathedral. Special medals were struck and prayers offered up for the health of the queen and the continuing independence of England. Elizabeth had survived her moment of greatest peril.

Unlucky voyage

One poor Spanish crew was shipwrecked on the Irish coast three times. After the first time, its crew joined a second Spanish ship in order to sail home. When that too was shipwrecked, the crew eventually joined up with a third ship. This time their luck ran out, as it too was shipwrecked with the loss of all 1,300 men on board.

November 1588
Elizabeth processes through London to a victory service at St. Paul's Cathedral.

1589, 1595, 1596, 1597
Further Spanish armadas and raiding parties against southern England are easily repelled.

GLORIOUS
QUEEN

Elizabethan England

Under Elizabeth, England prospered. Despite the threat from Spain, people had enough to eat, and trade and commerce grew. Above everything else, Elizabeth herself was loved and adored by her people.

One of the main achievements of Elizabeth's government was to reduce the religious arguments that had torn the country apart since the 1530s. She reintroduced Protestantism gently enough not to spark too much resistance. Her church still forms the basis of the Church of England today.

Throughout her reign, Elizabeth helped and supported merchants and traders in opening up new markets for English goods. She encouraged the Muscovy Company in its trade with Russia and, in 1600, gave a charter to a group of London merchants to begin a company to import spices from eastern Asia. The East India Company established bases in India, the start of an empire that in 200 years was to dominate the world.

Most people lived and ate well during Elizabeth's reign.

Previous page: Elizabeth is carried through the streets of London to Whitehall Palace around 1580.

Left: The finest Elizabethan music was heard in church, and the first recognizably modern hymns were being composed and sung.

1595
The first performances take place of William Shakespeare's *A Midsummer Night's Dream* and *Romeo and Juliet*.

1595
Rebellion breaks out in Ireland.

Above: At harvest time, everyone in the local area was expected to help bring the harvest in before the storms of autumn. The grain was then stored in barns for use throughout the year.

However, if the harvest was bad, food became scarce and expensive. Twice, Elizabeth's government introduced new laws to help people in times of hardship, one of the first examples of what is now called the "welfare state." For working people, life was hard. They worked long hours for little money, and had little time off. Sundays, holy days, and feast days, however, were causes of great celebration, with music, dancing, and other entertainments.

The longer she reigned, the more Elizabeth was respected and loved. Everyone knew what she looked like because her portrait hung in public buildings and private houses, and prints of her likeness were made for sale and display. For many people, she was Gloriana, the glorious queen.

1597, 1601
New laws are introduced to tackle poverty.

1598
Elizabeth's trusted adviser William Cecil dies.

Elizabethan London

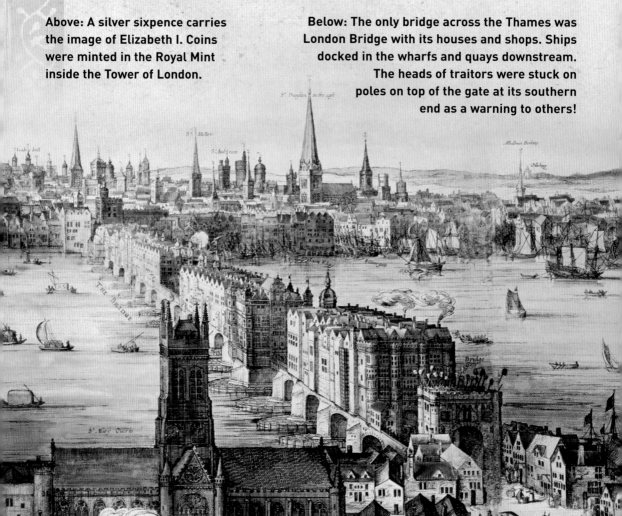

During Elizabeth's reign, London was by far the largest city in England, reaching a population of about 200,000 people by 1600. The city sat on both sides of the River Thames, a bustling waterway filled with ferries, water taxis, and boats bringing in goods from all over western Europe. The city was the royal, political, administrative, and legal capital of England. It was also its trading and commercial center. The streets bustled with merchants, shopkeepers, street-sellers, traveling actors and musicians, craftspeople, and numerous pickpockets and other criminals. Unfortunately most of the Tudor city was swept away in the Great Fire of London in 1666. But books, artifacts, paintings, and a few remaining buildings still give us a vivid picture of what Elizabeth's London was like.

Above: A silver sixpence carries the image of Elizabeth I. Coins were minted in the Royal Mint inside the Tower of London.

Below: The only bridge across the Thames was London Bridge with its houses and shops. Ships docked in the wharfs and quays downstream. The heads of traitors were stuck on poles on top of the gate at its southern end as a warning to others!

Above: Tudor London enjoyed bull- and bear-baiting, cock-fighting, and other sports now considered cruel. The bear was tied to a post and attacked by dogs. Sometimes its teeth were removed so that it could defend itself only with its paws.

Her Final Years

In 1600, Elizabeth had reigned for 42 years, much longer than her father or any other Tudor monarch, and was now 67 years old. Today, that is not considered an old age, but in Tudor times, she was thought to be very old.

Above: During her life, portraits of Elizabeth always showed her as a young woman. Possibly this unusual portrait was painted after her death.

During the last few years of Elizabeth's reign, poor harvests caused hardship across the country. Her favorite minister, William Cecil, died; a rebellion broke out in Ireland; and one of her courtiers, the Earl of Essex, tried to overthrow her government. Members of Parliament kept pressing her to name a successor.

In 1601, Elizabeth addressed her Parliament for the last time. In her farewell speech, she summed up her reign as queen and pledged her continuing love for her country and its Parliament. Still ruling as queen, eighteen months later, in March 1603, she took to her bed for the last time. According to the royal chaplain, Dr. Henry Parry, the queen had been "oppressed with melancholy" for two weeks and refused to eat or to "receive any physic [medicine]." On her last two days, she could not speak.

1600

Elizabeth grants a charter to the East India Company to trade spices and other goods with eastern Asia.

February 1601

The Earl of Essex, Elizabeth's favorite, leads a rebellion in London against her government.

At about 3 a.m. on March 24, Elizabeth died, "mildly like a lamb, easily like a ripe apple from the tree." Her funeral took place on April 28. A procession of 1,000 people escorted the coffin to Westminster Abbey, watched over by tens of thousands of grieving Londoners. She was buried under the main altar of the Henry VII chapel.

As the funeral took place, her chosen successor, James VI of Scotland and son of Mary Queen of Scots, was hurrying south from the Scottish capital, Edinburgh, to claim his throne. The queen was dead. Long live the king!

Last words

On November 30, 1601, Elizabeth addressed Parliament for the last time: "Though God hath raised me high, yet this I account the glory of my crown, that I have reigned with your loves.... It is not my desire to live or reign longer than my life and reign shall be for your good. You never had, nor shall have any that will love you better."

Below: Elizabeth's coffin was covered in purple velvet and escorted through the streets of London by earls and barons wearing black and carrying the banners of the Tudor family and kingdom.

November 1601
Elizabeth addresses Parliament for the final time.

March 24, 1603
Elizabeth dies quietly in Richmond Palace and is later buried in Westminster Abbey.

Elizabeth's Legacy

The death of Elizabeth marked the end of an era, as she was the last of the Tudor dynasty. After her death, the Stuart kings took over, and British history changed forever. But Elizabeth left a vast legacy for people today.

Above: Black-and-white wood-framed buildings are one of the most visible legacies of Elizabethan England. This house, in Wilmcote, Warwickshire, was once owned by Mary Arden, Shakespeare's mother.

The most important legacy of Elizabeth was that when she died there was no dispute about the succession. Her father's six marriages had caused dynastic chaos, and both Elizabeth and Mary had had to fight to become queen. But when Elizabeth died, James VI of Scotland took over peacefully and became James I of England. As a result, the two thrones of England and Scotland were united for the first time ever. A century later, in 1707, the two countries were united too, thus ending one of the most bitter, long-running feuds between neighbors in Europe.

July 1603
Elizabeth's successor, James I of England, is crowned in Westminster Abbey.

1879
The first Shakespeare Memorial Theatre opens in the Warwickshire town of Stratford-upon-Avon.

Right: The Globe Theatre on London's Bankside is an exact replica of a theater Shakespeare himself acted in until it was destroyed by fire after a performance of one of his own plays in 1613.

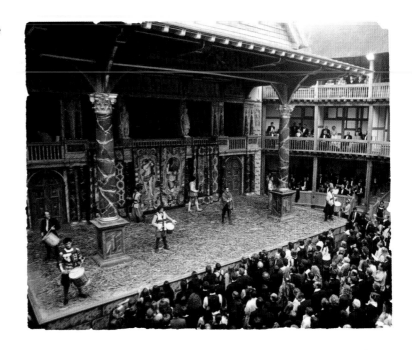

Elizabeth left James a strong government and a peaceful country. There had been no rebellions in England since 1569, and there were none again until 1642. Elizabeth also left the beginnings of a trading empire in India and a powerful navy that had just defeated the mightiest power in Europe and now controlled the seas. The capital, London, was rich as a result of trade and commerce. For its theaters and actors, William Shakespeare was writing the plays for which he would become the most popular and famous playwright of all time. His work is performed in theaters around the world today, and the English language owes much to Shakespeare.

But none of this would have been possible without the person of Elizabeth I, whose story this is. From her birth as a princess, hers is the amazing tale of how a young prisoner grew up to become the most famous queen in English history.

1952
The second Elizabethan age begins when Elizabeth II becomes Queen of the United Kingdom.

2003
The 400th anniversary of Elizabeth's death is commemorated with a major exhibition in Greenwich.

Glossary

abdicate to give up the throne, usually voluntarily.

adultery relationship between two people when one or both of them is married to somebody else.

alliance a partnership formed for the benefit of both parties.

ambassador the representative of a foreign country.

annul to cancel a marriage or other legal transaction.

armada a large fleet of warships; for example, the fleet sent against England by Philip II of Spain in 1588.

banquet a formal meal for many people.

bodice part of a woman's dress above the waist, sleeveless and often laced at the front.

bowls a game played on grass with wooden balls, which are rolled to stop as close as possible to a target ball.

Catholic person who is a member of the Roman Catholic Church and accepts the pope as head of that church.

charter a formal document from a monarch or head of state giving official approval to a new organization, for example a commercial company.

christening a Christian service at which a child is baptized—that is sprinkled with water as a sign that he or she is a member of the church—and is officially named.

circumnavigate to sail all the way around something, for example the world.

civil war a war that takes place within a country between two or more rival armies.

class a group of people of similar social and economic status.

colony a country or area under the control of another country and settled by people from that country.

coronation a ceremony at which a monarch is crowned king or queen.

courtier an attendant at the court of a king or queen.

divorce the legal recognition that a marriage has ended.

dynasty a family of hereditary rulers.

elect choose someone to hold public office by voting.

excommunicate to exclude someone from the Roman Catholic Church.

execute carry out a sentence of death on a condemned person.

galliard a lively dance in triple time performed by two people.

heir the male or female successor to the throne after the death or resignation of the current king or queen.

hereditary describes the passing down of a title or land from father to son or, sometimes, to daughter.

high treason a serious offense against the king or queen of a country, usually punishable by death.

house, royal a royal family.

illegitimate describes a child born of parents not legally married to each other at the time of the birth.

invasion the act of entering a country with an army in order to occupy or conquer it.

joust a combat with lances between two mounted knights.

lady-in-waiting lady of the royal household who attends and supports a queen or princess in her daily duties.

legitimate describes a child born to parents who are legally married to one another.

orb and scepter the jeweled globe and staff carried as symbols of authority by a king or queen.

pageant the outdoor theatrical performance of a historical scene.

Parliament, English the law-making institution in Westminster, London, consisting of an elected House of Commons and an unelected upper House of Lords.

pope the head of the Catholic Church, whose headquarters are at the Vatican in Rome, Italy.

Privy Council highest council of state in England, which advises the king or queen on government policy.

Protestant a Christian person who does not accept the supremacy of the Roman Catholic Church.

rebellion armed resistance to an established government or ruler.

Reformation, the a 16th-century religious movement that broke away from the Catholic Church and set up Protestant churches throughout Europe.

ritual a religious or solemn ceremony.

ruff a frill worn round the neck, as in Elizabethan England.

smallpox a very contagious (catching) disease with the symptoms of fever and sores; if the sufferer survives they will have many scars.

stepchildren the children by a previous marriage of a person's wife or husband.

symbol something that stands for or represents something else; for example, a scepter is a symbol of a monarch's power.

tournament sporting competition, originally designed as a training event for war, in which armored knights jousted against each other on horseback; by Tudor times the tournament was much more about display than combat.

tutor a private teacher, usually one who teaches a single pupil or a very small group.

welfare state a social system in which the government of a country takes responsibility for the health of its citizens.

Bibliography

Anne Boleyn: The Queen Who Lost Her Head, Beatty, Laura, published by Short Books, 2004

Children of England: The Heirs of King Henry VIII, Weir, Alison, published by Jonathan Cape, 1996

Kings and Queens: A Royal History of England and Scotland, Somerset Fry, Plantagenet, published by Dorling Kindersley, 1997

The Terrible Tudors, Deary, Terry, and Tonge, Neil, published by Scholastic Books, 1993

Tudor, Adams, Simon, published by Dorling Kindersley, 2004

Some websites that will help you to explore the Tudor period:

www.englishhistory.net/tudor.html
Biographies, portraits, questions, quizzes, and a detailed search engine to help you understand the Tudor period in more depth.

www.historyonthenet.com/Lessons/elizabeth1/eliz1main.htm
A look at the portraits Elizabeth commissioned of herself, and why and when they were painted.

www.pensacola.com/%7Erbethke/Armada.htm
Detailed account of the Spanish Armada, with a chronology of events, biographies of major participants, and numerous maps, pictures, speeches, and even recipes from the period.

www.royal.gov.uk/output/Page11.asp
The official website of the British monarchy provides biographies of all five Tudor monarchs, including Elizabeth I.

www.schoolshistory.org.uk/tudors.htm
A wide range of resources, pictures and student-friendly narratives about the Tudor period and its main events.

www.spartacus.schoolnet.co.uk/Tudors.htm
Numerous biographies, events, issues, and organizations from the Tudor period.

www.tudorhistory.org
Detailed website on Tudor history with sections including a who's who in Tudor history, life in Tudor times, Tudor architecture, family trees, detailed chronologies, and even something on Tudor humor and Tudors in the movies.

www.tudorplace.com.ar
Contains the Tudor family tree, biographies of famous Tudors, contemporary accounts of events and people, and much, much more.

Index

Acknowledgments

Sources: AA = The Art Archive, BAL = The Bridgeman Art Library.

B = bottom, T = top.

Front cover National Portrait Gallery, London, UK/Corbis; **1** BAL/Museum of London; **3** The Parochial Church Council of Preston St Mary, Suffolk, © The Friends of Preston St Mary Church, photography by David Emeney; **4T** The Royal Collection © 2004, Her Majesty Queen Elizabeth II (detail); **4B** The Royal Collection © 2004, Her Majesty Queen Elizabeth II (detail); **5T** AA/National Maritime Museum London/ Harper Collins Publishers; **5B** akg-images; **7** The Royal Collection © 2004, Her Majesty Queen Elizabeth II; **8** BAL/Hever Castle Ltd; **9** BAL/Mark Fiennes; **10** BAL/National Museums Liverpool; **11** The Royal Collection © 2004, Her Majesty Queen Elizabeth II; **12T** BAL/National Museums Liverpool; **12B** BAL/ Private Collection; **14** AA/Marquess of Bath/Eileen Tweedy; **15** Getty Images/Hulton Archive; **16** BAL/ Roger-Viollet, Paris; **17** BAL/Collection of the Earl of Pembroke; **18** Getty Images/Hulton Archive; **19** Getty Images/Hulton Archive; **20** BAL/Hatfield House; **21** Fotomas Index UK; **22** Corbis/© Art on File; **23** BAL/Lambeth Palace Library; **25** The Royal Collection © 2004, Her Majesty Queen Elizabeth II; **26** BAL/National Portrait Gallery, London; **27** Scala, Florence; **28** BAL/National Portrait Gallery, London; **30** *Queen Elizabeth I Dancing* reproduced by kind permission of Viscount De L'Isle, from his private collection at Penshurst Place; **32** BAL/© Yale Center for British Art, Paul Mellon Collection, USA; **33** BAL/Parham Park; **34** BAL/Private Collection; **35** Getty Images/Hulton Archive; **37** Staatliche Museen Kassel; **39** AA/National Maritime Museum London/Harper Collins Publishers; **40** BAL/© Glasgow City Council (Museums); **42** BAL/National Museums Liverpool; **43** BAL/Falkland Palace; **44T** AA/Cornelis de Vries; **44B** BAL/Victoria & Albert Museum; **45T** AA/British Museum/Harper Collins Publishers; **45B** BAL/National Portrait Gallery of Ireland; **46** AA/Eileen Tweedy; **48** BAL/Woburn Abbey; **51** akg-images; **52** Getty Images/Hulton Archive; **53** Fotomas Index UK; **54T** BAL/British Museum; **54B** BAL/ Private Collection; **55** BAL/Private Collection; **56** BAL/Phillips; **57** akg-images/British Library; **58** BAL; **59** Rex Features.